AF729235

cup

bell

gift

cloud

umbrella

vase

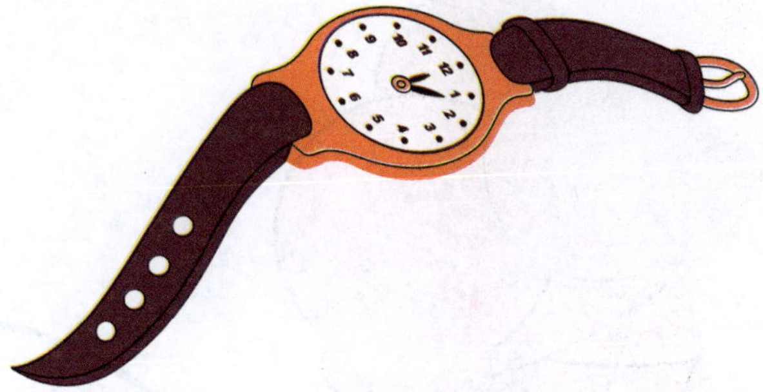

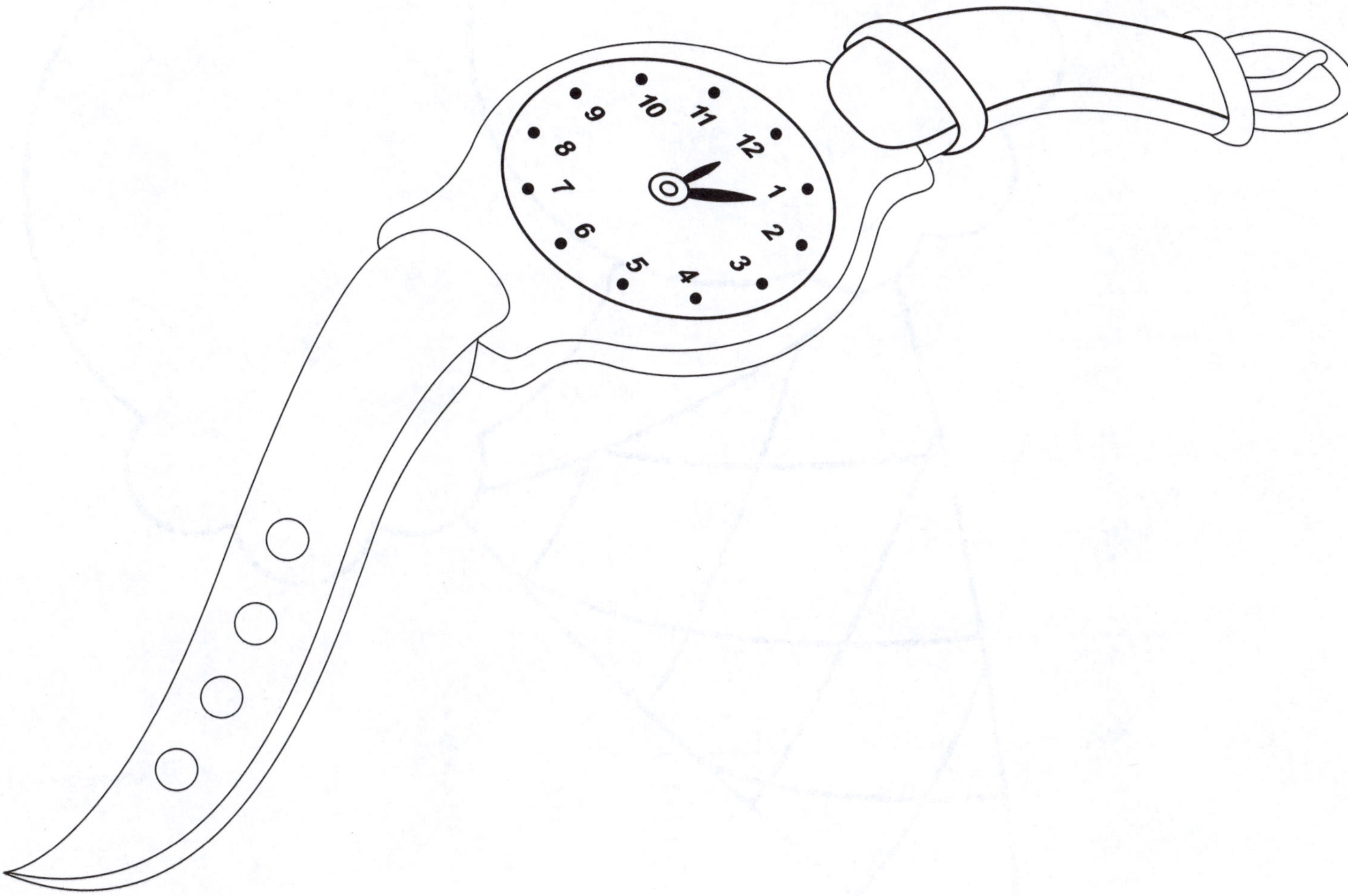

watch

ice cream

kite

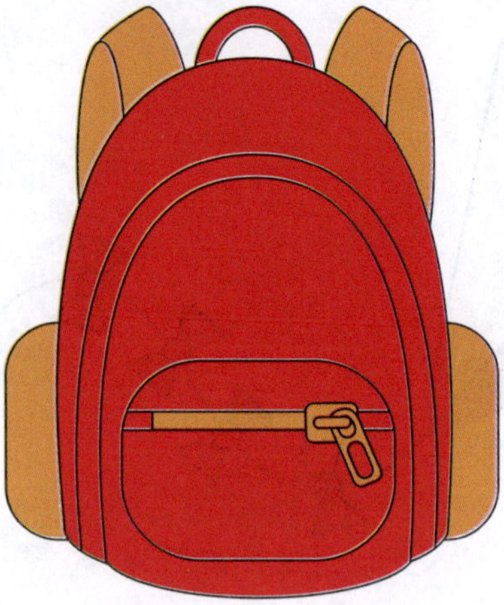

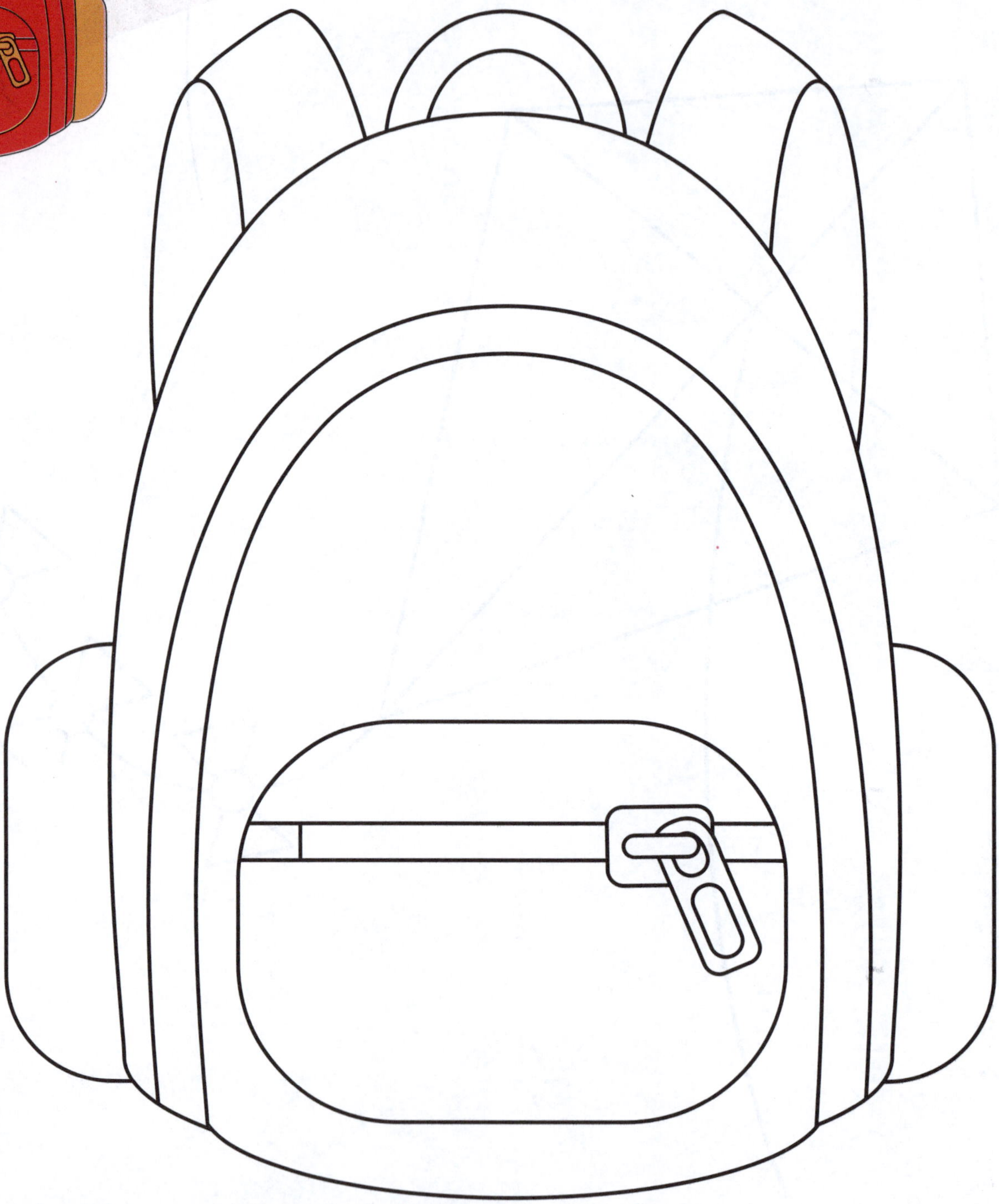

school bag

boat

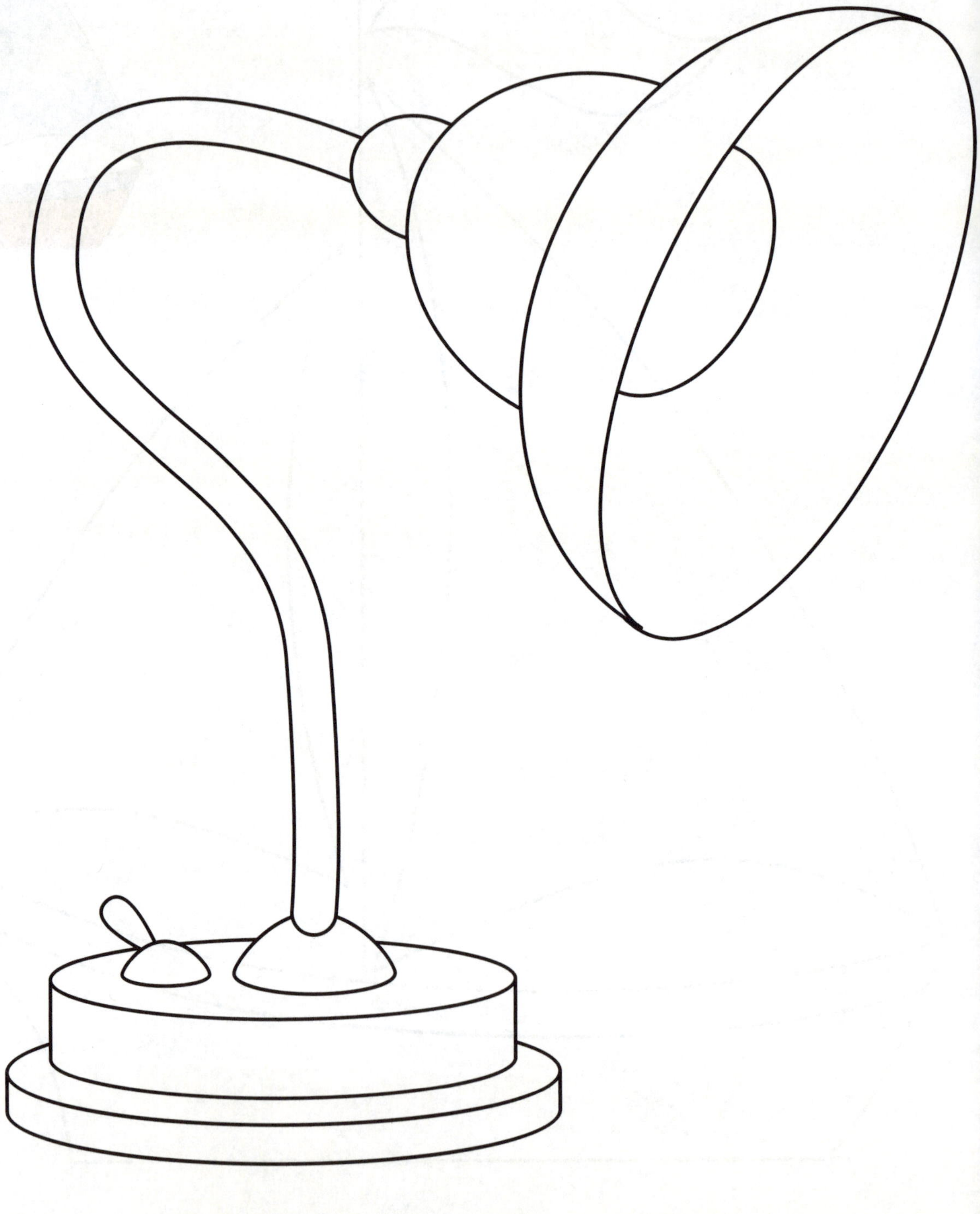

lamp

jug

truck

hot air balloon

book